The Secrets to Attracting Money Fast

I0492389

How to Successfully Build Your Money Consciousness

Thomas Fisher

Earnings Disclaimer

Every effort has been made to accurately represent this book and it's potential. In terms of earnings, there is no guarantees that you will earn any money using the techniques and ideas in this book. Information presented in this book is not to be interpreted as a promise or guarantee of earnings. Earning potential is entirely dependent on the person using this book's ideas and techniques.

Any claims made of actual earnings or examples of actual results can be verified upon request. Your level of success in attaining the results claimed in our materials depends on the time you devote to the program, ideas and techniques mentioned, your finances, knowledge and various skills. Since these factors differ according to individuals, we cannot guarantee your success or income level.

Many factors will be important in determining your actual results and no guarantees are made that you will achieve results similar to ours or anyone else. No guarantees are made that you will achieve any results from our ideas and techniques in our material.

<u>Dedication</u>

I dedicate this book to people who want to change their energetic frequency to money. To shift from just getting by to having more than enough!

*"Without a Rich Heart, Wealth
is an ugly beggar"*

— Ralph Waldo Emerson

Table of Contents

Introduction

Welcome to the secrets of attracting money fast. In this book you will learn the strategies and the process of being able to attract money indefinitely, and for as long as you need to, for the rest of your life.

You're going to learn how to transform your thoughts and feelings into manifested money into your outer physical experience. In this book, you will learn how to successfully create your money goals and set your money intention in which you will use, to maximize the attractive powers of your mind to manifest and attract money into your existence.

You will learn the principles of attracting money. The underlying principles that you will learn and master to empower yourself to always have the ability to attract money to you for the rest of your life.

You will learn the secrets of your subconscious mind. The ability for you to use and program

1

your subconscious mind, specifically for money, to attract money automatically into your outer physical reality.

You will learn the biggest secret to attracting money which is through your feelings. Your feelings and or emotions are the powerful attracting force, when cumulative, will allow you to build a combustion of energy which will allow for money to manifest itself and attract itself into your existence.

You will choose amongst a series of money affirmations and begin to utilize your selected affirmations to maximize your attracting power to attract money to you very fast.

You will develop a pattern of self-talk which you will repeat to yourself which will help to change the language pattern of your expectations of how frequent and how fast money flows into your life.

You will learn and master the art of expressing gratitude and appreciation in and around money. When you appreciate money and you are grateful for all the money that exists in the universe, you are sending out an extremely strong signal, which will allow for the attraction of money to flow quickly into your life.

You will develop a new and empowering money consciousness. I will give you the exact steps to follow to grow and develop your money consciousness. You will then establish and begin your Attract Money Fast Routine. This routine will be a new daily practice for you to maximize your money consciousness and your energetic frequency.

Between the development of your money consciousness and maximizing your energetic frequency, you will give yourself the ability to attract money very fast. Of course, you will need to read through this book and follow the steps and techniques that I lay out if you are to expect yourself to attract money fast.

I mentioned in the earnings disclaimer that there are no guarantees of exactly how much money you will earn reading and following the steps within this book, however the results can truly be unlimited. It is all up to you and your ability to master and fully utilize all the steps and processes within this book.

I included a bonus Chapter which will give you the initial steps to Money mastery. The initial foundation for you to grow and develop your own financial freedom. This bonus Chapter will give you this layout of instruction on how you can establish and build your financial foundation. This will help you on your path to achieving financial freedom.

If you are serious and really want to attract money fast, all of the steps within this book will give you exactly what you need. You will actually realize that the process can be really simple if you just simply follow the steps and techniques that are laid out within this book.

Shifting yourself from poverty to prosperity, you will learn how to empower yourself and your mind, and especially your ability to know precisely what it takes to manifest money into your life.

You have to believe that you can do it. Your

belief will be strengthened and developed thoroughly as you follow the steps and strategies within this book.

You also have to be willing to walk away from your current life's circumstances. Some people actually get stuck in poverty and they stay there. I can tell that by you purchasing this book, that you are serious and you are ready to start attracting money into your life.

Everyone deserves the good life. However very few know the secrets to what it takes to achieving infinite financial abundance. Your ability to absorb the knowledge within this book, and follow the steps that are within, will give you the ability to experience a level of infinite financial abundance in your own life.

So now let's move to chapter 1, where I will help you to establish your money goals and your specific money intention which will be the starting point for you to attract money fast.

You will then progress on to the next chapters, carefully underlining all of the most important points and steps to follow, so you can maximize your "Attract Money Fast Routine" and begin the process of attracting money fast into your life.

Chapter 1

Money Goals and Setting Your Intention

*"I am now attracting an
abundance of money, health,
and great people into my life"*

— John Assaraf

The first and most powerful step in the process of attracting money fast is to establish your money goals. As you list your money goals, you will then have the ability to create your main intention for attracting money fast.

Money goals can also be personal achievement goals. When you have decided that you want to attract money fast you will want to make a list of things that you will obtain when more money starts flowing into your life.

After all, money is simply a tool. Money is a

7

tool that we use to provide us with food, shelter, and possessions that give our lives more fulfillment. So, the first thing you'll want to do is to establish this list of things that you desire to obtain with more money as more money begins to flow into your life following the steps within this book.

Make a list now of the items that you would like to purchase when you have more money in your physical reality. Below is an example of some things that you may decide to put on your list.

A Larger Home
A Nicer Car
A More Extensive Wardrobe
More Vacations
Income Producing Assets
A New Watch
A New Boat

Some of these items listed above will give you a model you could work with when making your own personal list. Again, money is a tool. So, making this list is going to help you to grow and develop your money consciousness. When you know what you want, the universe allows for money to flow to you at a faster rate, than if you didn't know what you wanted.

So, it is important for you to know precisely what you want. Your money goal list is going to help you when you establish your Attract Money Fast Routine.

Once you are finished with your money goal list, you can then move on to establishing your money intention.

Your money intention is going to be your primary focus in your ability to attract money fast. And intention is a single pointed focus. So for the purposes of this book, you are going to establish a money intention that summarizes all of your money goals into one.

Think of your money intention as all of your money goals into one single focus. As it says in the Bible: "Seek ye first the kingdom of God, and his righteousness, and all these things shall be added unto you". What that means is that when you focus on the main source of money, wealth, and abundance, you will be tapping the main source of all riches.

Your single pointed focus on your established money intention will give you the ability to tap into the main source where all money flows from. As you exclusively focus on the main source of all abundance, the process of attracting money becomes the simplest.

If you were to put your energy into a less powerful source such as just focusing on your dream car, or your dream home, you would be limiting yourself to the all-powerful source where all wealth and abundance and money come from.

This is the starting point for you to start attracting money fast. You will establish your money intention and you will then utilize your money intention in your "Attract Money Fast Routine", which I will cover step-by-step in chapter 9 of this book.

There are a couple of ways to establish your money intention. Below I have provided a couple of examples.

Examples of Money Intentions

1. The entire universe is on my side, and is manifesting money into my existence

2. The source of all wealth and abundance is delivering money very fast into my life

3. Every person on this planet is a channel of money which can and will flow into my life

You can choose any particular money intention listed above as your primary money intention. You could also create a money intention of your own similar to the examples above.

The power behind the money intention, is for you **to utilize it in your daily routine, to maximize your focus on the biggest possible perceptions of money being able to attract itself into your life at the fastest rate possible.**

Think about the money intention in example number one above. **The entire universe is on your side and is manifesting money into**

your existence.

Really think about that statement. I will give you a little perspective on how big of a perception that is. Look around you, and at all the expensive items and things that money can buy in your reality. For example, look online for super yachts for sale. You will see some priced at around $50 million. Some larger ones will be in the hundred-million-dollar range.

In this example with the super yacht, you may think that that is a lot of money. The power of the intention in example number one above is infinitely more abundant than the super yacht.

In other words, your money intention is going to position you at full capacity in the ability to attract money fast into your life. When you entertain the perception of infinite abundance, and that means infinite amounts of money, you truly begin to vibrate at an infinite level, which allows for infinite levels of money to manifest into your life.

Your money intention is backed by two things. Your practiced perception of thinking and perceiving much larger money amounts then you could ever imagine. The second component is the feelings of infinite abundance and of attracting an infinite amount of money into your life.

This is a practice. You will be practicing this new expanding perception of infinite money and then expressing the feelings of what infinite money feels like to you.

This is the core component of your "Attract Money Fast Routine". This is the attracting power that you will be building within yourself, which will allow for money to attract very fast into your life.

Now let's further help you understand how powerful your created money intention will help you to attract money fact. In example number two of Money intentions listed above, which I also placed here below.

> *"The source of all wealth and*
> *abundance is delivering*
> *money very fast into my life"*

Pondering this statement allows for your imagination to entertain how powerful the source of all wealth can provide for you. The purpose of the money intention is for you to entertain a new perception of infinite reality. An infinite source that will deliver to you all the money you could ever desire.

Expanding your perception and expanding your imagination of just how powerful the universe is in its ability to attract money to you fast. Ponder the source of all wealth and abundance. Think about how big and powerful that source is. On top of the fact, it is an infinite supplier of all things good including money.

Think about that. **Feel the feelings of how powerful a source that the universe is to deliver money to you.** The practice of pondering and entertaining this perception and expanding your imagination and focusing in on the feelings of how powerful the source is, you are expanding your consciousness and increasing your energetic frequency.

Let's look at the money intention example

number three.

*"Every person on this planet
is a channel of money which
can and will flow into my
life"*

There are over 7.6 billion people on this planet. If you chose this money intention you would perceive and ponder 7.6 billion people that are an available channel to attracting money into your life.

Write out your money intention. You can use any of the three examples that I listed here. You can also create your own money intention. Once you have created your money intention you could then move on to chapter 2.

In chapter 2, I will be teaching you the principles of attracting money. Knowing the principles of attracting money, provide you with a full understanding of how the system of money works.

Specifically, how money works in the outer

world, and also how your inner world heavily determines exactly how much money you're going to manifest and attract into your life.

Chapter 2

The Principles of Attracting Money

*"There is no ending to the
inflowing of abundance, it is
like water ever flowing into
your life"*

— Abraham

Money is a powerful force. Money is also a symbol of energy and when you develop and maximize your money energy, you will allow for the attraction of maximum money into your life.

Money operates under certain universal laws and principles. I will be going over these laws and principles with you so you can master them and in return master your ability to attract and successfully manage money.

The outer principles of money mastery include

hard work, motivation and determination. These outer world physical principles are important for you to master in the art of making money.

Now with your inner world of consciousness, there are principles and laws which I will cover here to allow you to memorize and apply them into your ability to attract and make money.

Principle 1

Attention

Your focus and attention on attracting money needs to be very well disciplined. When you are focused on the intention of attracting money the universe will respond to you in proportion to your focus. Your focus and attention, also includes your expectation.

Expectations are focused thoughts into your main intention. The more you expect your intention to realize itself and manifest, the more power and attention you are sending out into the universe, to allow for the quickest and most profound manifestations of, in this case, money.

The Universe loves orderly and cleanliness. In regards to money, putting attention on the current money that you have, and to be organized in your money management, will allow the universe to be more open to delivering more money into your existence.

This can also be called creating a vacuum. In Catherine Ponders book "The Dynamic Laws of Prosperity", she talks about creating a vacuum. Creating a vacuum in this sense is to clean up and fully organize your financial matters. To be so well-organized, that you create a vacuum, a space allowing for more abundance to flow into your life.

The secret powerful way to attract and manifest anything is to create your intention and to then place as much attention on your intention until it manifests in your outer reality.

When you are consistent in placing attention upon your intention of attracting money fast, that focus will increase your expectations, and as you see evidence of synchronistic unfoldment, in increments of manifestation, you will further empower your manifestation and bring it to full realization.

Remember that attention and focus upon attracting money fast is one of the most powerful principles that you can use to achieve results and to manifest your desires in the quickest time possible.

Principle 2

Cleanliness & Organized

As I mentioned in principle one the universe loves cleanliness and order. Just like the many Universal Laws of the Universe, all of which are orderly and predictable. In regards to attracting money fast, cleanliness and being organized, will help to boost your ability to attract money fast.

In regards to cleanliness, you can begin by cleaning your home, your car, and any other thing that needs to be organized. This can be your email inbox or your prospecting list of people that are interested in your products and services.

You may have noticed in the past when your environment is clean and organized you feel much better. The power of cleanliness and being organized actually goes even deeper than that.

When you have a clean environment and an

organized environment you are again creating a vacuum to allow for more substance to come and manifest into your life. So, the trick to this principle is to make sure that you keep everything around you organized and clean.

This is one of the principles and strategies of attracting money fast. Each particular strategy and principle is equally important. In other words, to maximize your ability to attract money fast, you want to make sure that you are utilizing each and every principle that I lay out in this book.

Make a new habit of keeping your environment clean and organized and this will help you to begin the process of attracting money fast.

Principle 3

Circulation

Just like the universe is always in constant motion and constantly changing, you want to make sure that your money is circulating properly. If you hoard your money, and shove it in a box under your bed, it's not going to successfully circulate.

There is a flow to money. It's important to understand how this flow works. Sometimes money will flow into your life at a very fast rate. Other times money will flow into your life at a slower rate.

To master the money flow is to keep it circulating. When you pay your bills, you are circulating money back into the marketplace in return for the services that you are utilizing to help you manage your life.

When you make money, you also circulate your money by investing it into education, and investments to grow your money, and charitable donations. Yes, you are going to save some money in your bank account. However, you want to make sure that your money is circulating and working in your favor.

In regards to attracting money fast, when you have money circulating in an efficient manner then you can allow for the smooth manifestation of attracting money fast into your life.

One strategy I use with bills is to pay them right away. **The universe doesn't like procrastination**. If you are a procrastinator you will definitely want to work on fixing that. Procrastinators are usually unsuccessful people. So, this is a wake-up call for you to no longer procrastinate on anything in your life.

Arrange your finances and manage your money to where you can pay your bills the second that the bill arrives in the mail. This efficiency, of paying bills right away, allows for maximum money circulation in your life.

The same thing applies with making money.

As you are making money you want to have a plan for that money. When money comes in, and you already know where to circulate that money into, you will be maximizing your input to output of money circulation.

This principle of money circulation will eventually become an automated habit for you. Over time you will get better and better at circulating money at peak efficiency. This practice, this principle will give you the open flow of energy to maximizing your ability to attract money fast.

Don't be afraid to invest in yourself. When you purchase this book you invested into yourself and your financial future. Without realizing it you also have set the stage for maximum money efficiency. Your purchase of this book allowed for myself to earn a commission for providing you with fantastic information that can help you to get results and attract money fast.

At the same time your investment was also a highly efficient circulation of money because you have invested in yourself which will give you the tools and resources so you can attract money fast and therefore continue the flow of abundance throughout the entire universe.

Principle 4

Debt Owed and Due

This particular principle covers debt that you owe and also that that someone may owe to you.

When someone owes money to you is important to receive that money back in a timely manner. When that debt owed to you persists for too long, it affects the relationship you have with the person you lent the money to, and also with your thinking and pondering about when you're going to get the money back.

When you are waiting for someone to pay you back you're in a position and energetically in a space of lack. Because you are stressing, waiting for someone to finally pay you back, you're going to be in an energy frequency of lack.

So, make sure when you are lending money out, that they are reliable and honest and will pay you back in a timely manner. This maximizes the circulation of money and also keeps your energy level up to attract money fast at a high frequency of consciousness.

If you owe a person or company any money it is vitally important that you take the steps to paying back that debt in a timely matter. If you're unable to pay back that debt right away, then opt to do installment plans so you will eventually pay off your debt.

Some debt of course is good debt. This can be money that you borrowed from a bank to invest into a business or a real estate investment property. However aside from that, it is imperative that you work towards having next to no debt. Having little to no debt maximizes your energetic frequency to attract money fast.

Knowing that you don't owe anyone any money, and also realizing that you have next to little or no debt, really speeds up your energy and frequency allowing for maximum attraction powers of more and more money into your life.

Principle 5

Wasting Money on Unnecessary Things

One of the best ways of attracting money fast is to avoid overspending or wasting money on things that are completely unnecessary. Again, the universe likes cleanliness and order. In this regard with money, you will want to clean up your bad spending habits.

Don't buy anything that you don't really need. Don't spend money on things that are not going to help you to get you to the next level in your life. With money being such an important resource, and helping you to maximize your life experience, you will want to begin to develop a new habit of not wasting money.

You can take inventory on your money management and look for things that you are spending money on that are doing absolutely nothing to help your life improve and become more prosperous.

When you are wasting money or spending on

things that are completely unnecessary the universe begins to close its doors on bringing more money into your existence. This is what happens to lottery winners. They win an enormous amount of money and then they go and spend it on really stupid things.

Maximize this particular principle by being very careful of how you spend your money. You will find, over time, that your money spending habits will improve. The sooner they improve the better and the quicker you will begin to attract money fast.

Make sure to underline all of the important points that I cover within this book. When you reach the end of this book, start back at the beginning and review all of these principles and strategies. You will be utilizing them, altogether, to maximize your ability to attract money fast.

Principle 6

Creating a Prosperity Attitude

Your attitude is an expression of your energetic frequency of consciousness. Positive attitudes attract all good things, while negative attitudes attract all bad things. To maximize your ability to attract money fast you will want to develop a positive attitude.

This positive attitude doesn't necessarily mean dancing around a tree and saying I feel great, or I feel wonderful. What I mean by this positive attitude, specifically, is in regards to attracting money fast. Your attitude towards money itself is a critical component in attracting money fast.

This positive attitude also includes the positive approach to being willing to work hard and to positively believe that you can and will attract money fast.

Your attitude is an extension of your energetic frequency of consciousness. In my book, **The**

Secret Shift "How to Go from Talking about it to Being about it", I talk about the importance of focusing on thoughts and feelings to develop thoughtforms which begin to manifest into your character and thus your attitude and behaviors.

When you are focused on your money intention and you are paying attention to this intention on an everyday basis, you are focusing on how good it feels to have an infinite amount of money to start flowing into your life.

The more you practice this, the more your expectancy will become very positive. Your attitude will become positive as a result of this inner work. Utilizing all of the principles and strategies within this book you cannot but help to begin to develop a positive attitude.

There's no room for negativity and doubt and bad results. You're going to be so fixated on the strategies and principles within this book, and as you utilize them, your positivity is going to skyrocket.

People will begin to feel your positive energy

and will enjoy being around you. Your positive attitude will begin to open up the universal flow of all things good into your life.

Make sure you utilize this principle and maximize your ability to develop a positive attitude. You will be surprised at how quickly you will be able to attract money fast, when you incorporate a positive attitude into your routines, strategies, and principles within this book.

Principle 7

Generosity over Greed

Generosity and greed are two different perspectives that people tend to entertain. In regards to greed, you are focusing only upon yourself and your own needs.

When you make the transition from yourself to other people your energetic frequency is going to increase. When you are focused on servicing others and providing others with products that will benefit other people, you will begin to see more and more success and more prosperity flowing into your life.

> *"You will get all you want in life, if you help enough other people get what they want"*

— Zig Ziggler

When you are focused on serving people you are in the sweet spot of maximizing your ability to attract money fast. Take note that when you help enough people get what they want you will get what you want.

So, in your business, and in your ideas for products and services, and in your ability to manifest and attract money fast, you will want to focus on ways that you can help others with products, services, and inventions

This transition will pull you away from being greedy and cheap, and move you towards being generous, in your ability to solve problems and provide people with solutions to products and services.

Principle 8

Building on Accomplishments

As you are developing yourself, following the strategies and principles within this book, you will start to see some results slowly coming into your physical reality. In your journey of attracting money fast you are going to start to notice money showing up.

As you follow the steps and strategies within this book, and you start to see money attracting into your life, you want to record the results as they flow into your life.

When you are tracking the results, there are two things that are going to happen. Number one your expectation levels are going to increase. You're going to begin to expect more and more money to flow into your life. Number two you will be building upon the accomplishments and success of money flowing into your life.

Now, let's move on to chapter 3 where you will

learn about the power of your subconscious mind in its ability to help you attract money fast.

Chapter 3

Attracting Money with Your Subconscious Mind

"As you sow in your subconscious mind, so shall you reap in your body and environment"

— Joseph Murphy

Your subconscious mind is extremely powerful. The subconscious mind holds all of your belief systems from all of your life experiences up to this point. The goal of attracting money fast is to simply fill your subconscious mind with proper thinking and expectation of receiving large amounts of money.

Throughout this book, you have learned and will learn the many different strategies, and steps to follow to attract money fast. Almost all of these steps and strategies are working towards programming your subconscious mind to allow you to attract money fast.

You have a conscious mind and a subconscious mind. Your conscious mind is your rational thinking mind. It is also your left brain which is in charge of logical thinking. You are in control of your conscious mind and through your conscious mind you send commands to your subconscious mind.

The subconscious mind is more automatic. Meaning, that when your conscious mind programs your subconscious mind, the subconscious begins to manifest and bring life circumstances into your reality that match what you have been feeding to your conscious mind.

So, in order to control your life and master the law of cause and effect, you'll want to be very careful at what your conscious mind is being exposed to. You also want to be careful at what you're choosing to think and believe in your conscious mind. Just as the law of cause and effect states whatever your conscious mind thinks and believes (cause) enters your subconscious mind and becomes manifested circumstances in your life (effects).

Your subconscious mind is awake and alert 24 hours a day, seven days a week. The subconscious is always ready to receive commands on the fly. This means that when you start to make changes in your conscious thinking, your subconscious as a result, will begin to make changes in what manifests into your life.

This is a very inspiring fact that you can, at any given time, change the course and direction of your life. By flooding your conscious mind with the thoughts, and feelings which become beliefs, your subconscious mind will begin to manifest those thoughts and feelings that you are regularly entertaining on a daily basis.

One of the simplest ways to program your subconscious mind to attract more money to you, in a fast way, is to repeat the word "Wealth" to yourself every night before you go to sleep.

The subconscious is easiest to influence just before going to sleep and also just upon waking up in the morning. When you repeat the word wealth before you go to sleep you will be instilling a command into your subconscious mind.

The subconscious mind gets programmed through repetition. As you are repeating the word wealth over and over again, on a daily basis at night right before you go to sleep, you will be successfully programming your subconscious mind to focus on the word wealth. This will help to program the subconscious mind to allow you to manifest more wealth in your life.

There are other words and statements that you can repeat to yourself before you go to sleep. I will list a few of them below.

More Words & Statements You Can Repeat

Before Sleep:

More Money
Financial Abundance
I Am Attracting money

Choose one word or statement and repeat it to yourself for at least five minutes each night right before you go to sleep.

Now this strategy can be considered self-talk and also an affirmation. Throughout the day you can also repeat self-talk statements and affirmation statements. In my book: The Secrets of Creative Self-Talk, I cover self-talk much more in depth and how you can create your own self talk routine.

The next strategy to program your subconscious mind to attract money fast is to feel as if you are now receiving large amounts of money. The feeling itself is the emotion which is how the universe communicates. The Universe communicates through energetic frequency. Your emotions are energetically charged frequencies.

When you focus on the emotions of already having the thing that you want, that thing will begin to manifest itself into your life. You are sending out an emotionalized energetic frequency that matches how you want to feel when you already have received the thing that you want.

The subconscious mind works best through emotion. In regards to the subconscious mind, when you are focusing on thoughts that bring desirable emotions, and focusing on those emotions, you are successfully programming your subconscious mind.

As long as you are consistent and stick to a daily routine, of at least a half-hour each day, you will be successfully and consistently sending out the emotionally charged frequency of feelings of how you would feel when you already received what you desire.

The next step in programming your subconscious mind for attracting money fast is to be grateful for the money that you have right now. Even if you have very little money in your bank account you can be grateful that you have it.

The focus of gratitude and feeling appreciative of what you currently have sends a signal to the subconscious mind to allow for the manifestations of more things to be thankful for.

Gratitude is a very powerful emotionally charged frequency. The frequency of gratitude is very similar to the frequency of love. Both of these frequencies are extremely powerful in helping you to raise your energetic frequency which will allow for more desirable things to attract and flow into your life.

The next step in programming your subconscious mind is to feel that you deserve to have a lot of money. In order to attract money fast and bring money into your life you need to feel as if you deserve it. The universe itself is infinitely abundant.

This means that there is an infinite amount of money currently existing in our world. The amount of money that exists in our world is always increasing. You yourself are an individualization of the creator. There is a piece of the God force inside of you. Therefore, you are entitled to an abundance of all things good.

You are entitled as long as you believe that you are entitled. In in the outside world you will line yourself up with ways to make money that best suit your talents and abilities. Within your mind feeling entitled gives your subconscious mind the command that it is okay for you to have an abundance of money.

Another powerful strategy for programming your subconscious mind to attract money fast is to be grateful and thankful for people around you and people that you see on television that have a lot of money.

To be grateful for people that are currently rich and wealthy tells your subconscious mind that it is okay and acceptable. This gives your subconscious mind the ability to allow the same circumstances to be rightful for you.

So always be grateful when you see a wealthy

person. A great piece of advice is if you're able to talk to them is to ask them how they became rich and wealthy. Always be studying people that make large amounts of money. The more you study how money and wealth is generated the more you will know precisely how to go about generating large amounts of money and wealth.

Now when I mentioned entitled above, that doesn't mean that you can sit back and relax and let your subconscious mind bring money to you. Entitlement in the outer world of reality is not good unless you are achieving and producing products and services for improving people's lives.

The trick to entitlement is to be thoroughly focused on how you can service people through products and services. As you are servicing mankind entitlement becomes automatic.

Imagination is another powerful tactic with the subconscious mind. Imagining wealth and financial freedom will feed your subconscious mind to allow the manifestation of money and wealth to come into your life.

Imagine that you hold the same thoughts and beliefs as the wealthiest people on the planet.

Imagine what that would feel like. Transcend yourself through imagining what the richest people on this planet think about and believe. As you are imagining this you will begin to entertain thoughts and beliefs that are this level of consciousness.

Here's another one...

Imagine that you are capable of doing anything and that you are fearless in taking calculated risks and confident that you can achieve what you set out to accomplish.

Imagining these particular traits of believing you are capable of doing anything and being fearless in your execution of taking calculated risks. This is going to build your confidence and as you imagine it your subconscious mind start to believe that this is true for you. This is a powerful way to grow and develop your self-image

Your self-image is stored in your subconscious mind. So, as you are working with the strategies here to program your subconscious mind, you are growing and developing a self image which is expanding and moving towards the person that you ultimately will become.

As you are developing your self-image you will be aligning yourself with your desires and in this case the desire of attracting money fast.

Here's a really powerful one…

Imagine what your life would be like if you can afford to buy anything you desire.

This is a very powerful use of your imagination. Imagine if you had all the money in the world, an unlimited supply of money, what would you buy? When you are imagining a scenario like this you are feeding your subconscious mind with the possibility of having an unlimited amount of money.

To feed your subconscious mind with the idea that you have an infinite amount of money, you truly are aligning your subconscious mind with infinite wealth. The daily practice of this imagination will fortify the subconscious mind to allow for the manifestations of more money and abundance to come into your life.

Always remember that it is the thoughts and feelings that program your subconscious mind. Your outer reality will not change until you change your interior mind and consciousness.

Money is not going to attract itself to you fast if your current subconscious mind is filled with poverty and lack thinking. The most important take away from this book is for you to realize that you have to do your inner work of programming your subconscious mind to allow for changes to happen in your outer reality.

As the saying goes: "The Rich get Richer"

What exactly does this statement mean? This statement could be the summary of this book in one statement. What I mean by that is that as you are following the steps and strategies within this book you will put yourself in that same position to prosper over and over again.

The rich get richer because the subconscious mind of a rich person is filled with money, abundance, and all things good. The statement also means that once you begin to generate momentum of attracting money into your life, you will begin to prosper and accumulate more money and wealth. As you do that your thoughts and feelings will reinforce your subconscious mind to continue the process.

Therefore, as you begin to get rich and wealthy by programing your subconscious mind, you will begin the process of momentum which will continue to repeat itself indefinitely.

Of course, you will need to stay consistent in these thoughts and beliefs. You should always be on your guard from poverty thinking and poverty consciousness.

No matter how wealthy you become poverty will always exist in this world. In certain poverty-based habits such as overspending, wasting money, and getting into bad investment opportunities, will pull you away from the momentum of staying wealthy and perpetuating wealth in your life.

This summarizes the strategies in which you can program your subconscious mind to attract money fast

Make sure to underline each step and strategy that I have covered within this chapter. You will be utilizing them in your Attract Money Fast Routine. By the time you reach chapter 9, you will be ready to begin your Attract Money Fast Routine.

Now let's move to chapter 4 in which I have dedicated one full chapter to the focus of feeling your way to attracting money fast.

Chapter 4

Feel to Attract Money Fast

"Money is just energy. Let it flow"

— Mark Attwood

I dedicated a full chapter to the process of "feeling your way" to attracting money fast. The universe consists of energy and frequency. Your thoughts give birth to emotions which are energy in motion. The ability to feel the emotions of how it would feel if you had money coming to you easily and quickly, will allow you to attract money fast.

The process of entertaining the thought of attracting money fast, and then feeling how good it would feel, for you to receive money quickly and consistently on a regular basis. The feeling is the emotion which sends the signal out into the universe.

As you are consistent, on a daily basis, your practiced daily emotionally charged feelings will help you to maximize your ability to attract money fast.

They say, **"Feeling is the Secret,** and it truly is. That you entertain emotions which manifest circumstances into your life. **However, you can't manifest anything unless you are consistent with similar emotionally charged feelings on a regular basis.**

Consistency is the key. In your Attract Money Fast Routine, you will be practicing the thoughts of receiving money quickly and easily. As you feel so you shall experience the consistent and practiced feelings and emotions that you send out to the universe.

In your everyday life you can now pay attention to how you are feeling. Since your subconscious mind and the universe are always receiving signals from you on what to manifest into your life, you should always be on your guard, to pay attention to how you feel.

The ability to control your emotions, now

knowing that your emotions are signals sent out to the universe to manifest reality for you, you can now truly gain control over your life and over the circumstances, that will be manifesting into your life right now and very soon into the future.

So, when you are doing your daily Attract Money Fast Routine, throughout the rest of the day, you will want to also make sure that you are vibrating at a frequency that allows universe to deliver money and abundance into your life.

There is power with consistency. When you stay consistent in the emotions that you choose to focus on each day, you will maximize the momentum power of being able to attract money to you fast.

To attract money fast, your state of mind needs to be consistently focused on the thoughts and feelings of attracting large amounts of money, and also the feelings of gratitude, of having the money that you currently have.

Stay away from anyone that talks negatively

about money. Stay away from poverty thinking and poverty circumstances. When you are consistent in thinking and feeling the thoughts and feelings of having infinite amounts of money, you give yourself the best odds at manifesting money into your life at the quickest rate possible.

If you let things get into your way such as negative thinking, being around people that speak of poverty, you will slow down the process of being able to attract money fast.

When you stay consistent, on focusing on prosperity, abundance, and having an infinite amount of money in your possession, you will truly align yourself with infinite abundance.

This is a discipline that you will develop. In fact, the discipline of staying consistent in your thoughts and feelings, on having any expectations of receiving an infinite amount of money, is even more important than your physical work at obtaining the money.

Yes, you will need to work to accumulate money. **You don't have to work hard. You**

can simply work smart. However, the most important aspect of attracting money to you fast is your ability to align yourself with the emotions of what it feels like to have an infinite amount of money, and to expect that opportunities and money are going to flow into your life.

To be able to stay consistent with this frame of thinking and feeling will give you total power in your ability to attract money fast.

By now, I hope you have learned and realized how important the feeling and emotion is, in your communications to the universe, to attract the things that you want to manifest into your life.

The strategy of thinking a desirable thought to bring on an emotionally charged feeling, as if you have that thing now, is a practice that you will grow and develop into. This strategy needs to be developed.

This means that right out of the gate, you may not have the ability to fully believe and to practice thoughts and feelings of manifesting things that you desire. Over time, you will begin to develop your ability to think, and to feel and focus in, on the feeling of having a thing that you desire as if you already have it now.

You will eventually master your ability to get into the thinking and then the feeling of already having your desire, which will allow you to speed up the manifestation of your desire

Here's an example of how the strategy works:

You find a quiet place, undisturbed, and you decide to think about something that you desire. As you are thinking of this desire, begin to feel the feelings and focus on the emotions of how you would feel, if you already had this desire in your life.

It is at this point in the process, that you will be growing and developing, your ability to send the most efficient signals to the universe.

When you begin to focus on the emotions and feelings of already having your desire you will be thinking of a scale of 1 to 10. An emotional scale of 1 to 10. On this scale you will measure how strong your emotionally charged feeling is. Your work will be to increase the emotionally charged feeling working it up to a 10 out of the 10.

As you are doing this work, to raise the frequency of your feelings of having your desire, as if you have it right now, the signal that you send out to the universe will grow stronger and stronger.

Eventually, your ability to think a thought of something you desire and bring on an emotion at a 10 out of the 10, you will become an expert at manifesting things into your life.

In regards to attracting money fast, you will think the thoughts of having an infinite amount of money flowing into your life right now, and then entertaining the feelings of how good that feels, to be receiving and accumulating an enormous amount of money.

The paragraph above, covers the precise strategy of attracting money fast into your life. To think the thoughts of receiving an infinite amount of money and in matching your thought with feelings and emotions of receiving an infinite amount of money, aligns yourself to the universe to receive an infinite amount of money.

Don't let anything get in your way. Stay focused and stay consistent. Your consistent and daily practiced emotions and feelings, of already receiving large amounts of money, gives you the best communication with the universe to allow for the manifestation and ability to attract money fast into your life.

Reread this chapter to make sure that you understand the importance, and the power behind the feeling and the emotions of feelings, as if you already have the thing that you desire.

Most importantly, to stay consistent and to focus on thoughts that bring on desirable feelings and emotions of already having your desire on a daily basis. This assures that you are working to align yourself with the frequency of financial abundance.

In order to allow for the best manifestations,

consistency is of the uttermost importance. In your Attract Money Fast Routine you will b following the strategies and steps within thi book to maximize your ability to attract money fast.

This is a daily focus in a daily routine that you will be following. The question is how bad do you want to attract money fast? The answer and your ability to attract money fast, rests in the discipline of you conducting your daily Attract Money Fast Routine, and staying consistent every day, to assure that you have aligned yourself properly, to allow for the maximum manifestation of attracting money to you fast.

Now we can move to chapter 5 where we will go over the different affirmations that you can use, and the particular strategies of how to use them, in your persuit attracting money fast

Chapter 5

Attracting Money with Affirmations

*"Money Flows to me easily
and effortlessly"*

— Thomas Fisher

Affirmations are statements, that you repeat to yourself, to allow to sink into your subconscious mind. There are a few different strategies, on how to use affirmations, to allow for you to attract money fast and to manifest any desire into your life.

In this chapter, I will be presenting you with a good number of money affirmations, to allow you to choose at least three and begin to use them on a daily basis. There are different ways in which you can use these affirmations and I will go over those for you right now.

One way is to simply state the affirmation

repetitively for five minutes each day. Another strategy is to record your voice reciting the affirmation with gentle background music. You can listen to this audio recording first thing in the morning and right before you go to sleep. The audio recording of your affirmations only needs to be about five minutes in length.

Another strategy is for you is to write down your affirmation about 10 to 15 times each day. When you are writing your affirmation down you are thinking about the affirmation and the emotions of how you would feel if that affirmation was true.

When you are repeating the affirmation, you are programming your subconscious mind. Through repetition, you will have the ability to program your subconscious mind, and the affirmation will become a vital tool, in allowing for you to create change within your subconscious mind, and then in your outer physical reality.

Let's now go over a series of money affirmations for you to choose from. You can start with three and you can work with up to three affirmations for 21 days. You can then select three other affirmations to repeat for 21 days. A variety of affirmations will allow your subconscious mind to be thoroughly programmed with money attracting affirmations which will allow you to attract money fast.

Here is the list of effective Money Affirmations:

I love money and money loves me

I am receiving money now

I have more than enough money

I am grateful for what I already have and for all that I received now

My income is growing higher and higher

I have the power to attract money

Money flows to me easily

My bank balance is increasing every day and I always have enough money for myself

The universe is the constant supplier of money for me and I always have enough money to fill my needs

Every day I am attracting and saving more and more money

My money consciousness is always increasing and keeping me surrounded by money

I am focused on becoming rich

Attracting money is easy

Money is energy and my emotions of feeling wealthy will attract money to me

My wallet is overflowing with money

My pockets are full of money

I can always get whatever I need

There is enough money for everyone

Money flows easily into my life

Money flows to me easily, frequently, and abundantly

I place no limits on the amount of money I can make

My bank account is filled with money

I have an endless supply of cash

I attract money everywhere I go

Today is the day of my amazing good fortune

I am now accumulating large sums of money

I am increasingly magnetic to money

Money comes to me easily and effortlessly

A constant flow money is coming to me from known and unknown sources

Money flows freely into my life

All the money I need is flowing to me

Money now comes to me in abundance in perfect ways

Money flows to me like a waterfall

Of course, there are more money affirmations available, but I am sure that you can select three good ones from the list above.

Once you have selected your three affirmation you will then utilize them in your Attract Money Fast Routine. When you get to chapte 9, you will be able to set up your Attract Money Fast Routine, and begin the process o attracting money fast.

Now let's move the chapter 6 where you wil learn how to effectively use self-talk for th purposes of attracting money fast.

Chapter 6

Self-Talking Your Way to Attracting Money

"Relentless, repetitive self-talk is what changes your self-image"

— Denis Waitley

Self-talk, similar to affirmations, are statements that you repeat to yourself about yourself. You'll hear some people say "just my luck", or "these things always seem to happen to me". Those two particular self-talk examples are negative self-talk statements.

Self-talk can be empowering when you are using it in a positive way. **Self-talk also becomes powerful when it is repetitive and used on a daily basis**. To learn more about the in depth understanding of self-talk you can refer to my book: The Secrets of Creative Self-

Talk, "How to Talk Your Way into Wealth, Health, and Prosperity".

For the purposes of this book, I am going to give you some powerful self-talk statements that you can repeat to yourself specifically used to attract money fast. You will be utilizing this particular strategy of self-talk in your Attract Money Fast Routine.

Self-Talk Statements for Attracting Money Fast:

I always find the best ways to make money

Money is easy to make and I always have a lot of money in my bank account

I am very lucky because I attract money every day

Things are working out for me and I'm always making more money

Things seem to go my way and I am grateful that I am finding the ways to make large amounts of money

People like me and want to do business with

me

People love my products and services and want to buy them

I'm grateful that things always work out in my favor

I am comfortable with receiving large amounts of money

I feel great and every day my income increases

I am finding the next idea for a household product to sell

I am confident I am wealthy and I have multiple streams of income

The tellers at the bank know my name

I always get the best deals when I buy things that I need

I am always in control of my life and I succeed on a daily basis

Money and I are best friends

Abundance is natural for me and I receive it

every day

Prosperity is my birthright. I deserve prosperity and I receive it daily

The more I feel rich the more I will get rich

The more money that comes to me the more I attract even more

Quickly and easily money flows into my life

Money is always flowing to me

I'm the type of person that was meant to be rich

You can utilize any and all of the self-talk statements above, to help you in building your self-image and your relationship with money. Self-talk statements can be recorded and listened to on a daily basis even just for five minutes per day.

The goal with self-talk is for you to memorize at least 3 to 5 self-talk statements that you can repeat yourself throughout the day. This repetition will help you to develop your self-image.

Affirmations are very powerful at reprogramming your subconscious mind. Self-talk statements allow you to reinforce your affirmations, for even more stronger programming of your subconscious mind, to achieve results. Self-talk is another powerful routine that you will be using in your Attract Money Fast Routine.

Let's now move to chapter 7 where we will talk about money gratitude and appreciation.

Chapter 7

Money Gratitude and Appreciation

"Gratitude is riches.
Complaint is poverty."

— Doris Day

Gratitude and appreciation are powerfu
attracting emotions that attract all things gooc
into your life. The more grateful you are, fo
what you have, and also being grateful for the
infinite abundance of the universe, allows the
manifestation of more infinite abundance tc
flow into your life.

In regards to money, and especially attracting
money fast, you will be utilizing the powerful
resource of gratitude and appreciation in your
Attract Money Fast Routine.

Gratitude and appreciation, when utilized
properly, can allow you to attract money fast.

The most powerful way to utilize gratitude and appreciation is to spend 30 minutes per day, undisturbed and while listening to relaxing music, focusing on the gratitude and appreciation of how powerful the universal source is in delivering all good things to your life.

When you are conducting this session of 30 minutes of gratitude and appreciation, you will shift your emotions to 100% gratitude and appreciation. You will feel the emotional energy of these two powerful forces, which will bring you into an energetic frequency, that is extremely receptive to all things good.

As you practice this routine, you will begin to feel the power of gratitude and appreciation. This is an extremely important practice in your Attract Money Fast Routine. The real secret to attracting money fast is your ability to raise your consciousness to an energetic frequency that is more in alignment with the universal source of infinite abundance.

The more you align yourself with the universal

source of infinite abundance, the more you will be able to attract money fast. The daily practice of shifting and focusing your emotions into gratitude and appreciation, for not just money, but also for all things good, will put you in the energy space to attract the best and most desirable things in your life.

While you are also in your 30-minute routine of daily gratitude and appreciation, another technique is to focus on how grateful you would feel if you had an amount of money in the bank that would make you feel amazing. Feel the feelings of gratitude and appreciation of how good and grateful you feel for having the money in your possession in your bank account right now.

The trick to igniting the power of emotions of gratitude and appreciation is to truly feel that you have the thing you desire right now. With each day, as you practice your gratitude and appreciation focusing, along with the rest of the steps and techniques within the attract money fast routine, you will fortify yourself with maximum power in your ability to attract money fast.

In regards to gratitude, throughout your daily life, you will want to start to pay attention to the world around you and how you choose to react to it. When you start your day and finish your day with gratitude and appreciation, you consistently upgrade your energetic frequency of consciousness.

The more you desire to attract money fast the more you will utilize the conscious control of how you choose to express your emotions on a day-to-day basis. Choose gratitude and appreciation over complaining and being negative.

The universe functions on gratitude, and appreciation, and love. The universe is in automatic delivery mechanism always giving to you what you are sending out to it initially. What I mean by this, is that it is your responsibility to send out the right signal of emotion, in order for the universe to deliver to you the desirable things that you want to come into your life.

If you are complaining, or if you are feeling as if you lack money, and as if you don't have enough money in the bank, you're going to attract more lack and poverty in your life.

When you line yourself up with gratitude and appreciation you allow the universe to do its job in delivering prosperity and the things you desire into your life.

When you see a wealthy person driving a fancy car express appreciation for that person and that nice car that they are driving. Appreciate all things good, and express your emotions of appreciation, when you see things that you desire to attract into your own life.

Appreciation of people, desirable material items, vacations, the beautiful rose garden, and all the other things that you can appreciate, help you to align yourself with that energy of appreciation which will allow the universe to deliver future life experiences that will allow for more appreciation.

Think of each action you take, each thought and emotion you feel, as a feedback loop with the universe. Everything you give out in your thoughts, your emotions, your habits and behaviors, are all a language that you are speaking to the universe. Through this loop, you then receive similar and like experiences that match what you are giving out.

The majority of the world population live in the consciousness that is more poverty stricken then the small percentage of the population who live in abundance and gratitude.

When you make the shift into gratitude in abundance, you will be raising your consciousness and moving your life circumstances and manifestations into more desirable outcomes. You will be moving into the small percentage of population on this planet that consistently live in prosperity and abundance.

Two great things happen when you achieve this. Number one, you will be able to achieve all of your personal goals and manifest the conditions and things that you desire. Number two, you will be able to give back to the world.

As a spiritual being you are connected to all other beings on this planet. Of course, you want to achieve your own personal goals. However on top of this, one of the greatest things you can do when you achieve your ideal life is to devote time to help the lives of others. To help others to achieve their own ideal life.

The more you focus on gratitude and appreciation, the more you will become a loving force for the planet as a whole. So getting back, you want to incorporate gratitude and appreciation into your Attract Money Fast Routine.

Make sure that you fully understand this chapter and reread it to make sure that you have it thoroughly understood within your mind and memory. You want to begin to incorporate gratitude and appreciation into your daily life. The emotions of gratitude and appreciation are extremely powerful and they will help you to attract money fast.

The outside world will try to pull you away from gratitude and appreciation. The average person usually speaks negatively about things. The average public conversation is usually negative. So, it is of vital importance that you recognize the negativity that exists around you and to disregard it.

Instead, you will be choosing gratitude and appreciation as your new regularly practiced emotions. This will shift the frequency of who you are as an energetic being. This will give you the power to attract money fast, when you successfully align yourself with this new energy of gratitude and appreciation, practiced on a daily basis.

Let's now moved to chapter 8 where you'll be learning how to attract money through the development of your money consciousness.

Chapter 8

Attracting Money Through the Development of Your Money Consciousness

Your money consciousness is the accumulation of your thoughts feelings and especially your belief systems in relations to money. In this chapter you are going to learn how to grow and develop your money consciousness. When you begin to follow your Attract Money Fast Routine, you will be utilizing the steps and strategies to allow you to attract money fast.

More importantly, your Attract Money Fast Routine will be helping you to develop your money consciousness. In this chapter I'm going to talk about the most important and core components for the development of your money consciousness.

You will also learn precisely what to avoid to keep your consciousness from falling into a poverty-stricken consciousness. When you have put in the daily efforts of practicing your Attract Money Fast Routine, you will grow and develop a powerful money consciousness.

This newly developed money consciousness will automatically shift your awareness toward abundance and prosperity. You will naturally expect and attract money into your life on a regular basis.

As you maintain your powerful money consciousness you will consistently and continuously attract money into your life. It is your responsibility to make sure that your consciousness continues to stay grounded in prosperity and financial abundance.

Let's now go over the core components that you need to follow and master to grow and develop a powerful consciousness that will attract money to you fast.

Pay Attention to Your Thoughts and Words

The first component is to watch your thoughts and words carefully. Pay attention to your attitude towards money and to those people who are wealthy and abundant. If you talk about poverty and lack you will manifest lack in your life.

If you resent people who have money you will push money away from you. The subconscious mind is always listening to the conscious mind. Always remember that what you focus on you manifest. So be very careful with your thoughts and words. Instead of saying things like "I can afford it", change that statement to "how can I afford it?"

In this component, this is where the power of self-talk and affirmations come in handy. When you are utilizing effective self-talk statements and affirmations you will gradually overpower any poverty-stricken thoughts and words in your vocabulary.

As you make this shift from poverty to prosperity, from negative to positive, you will be building a powerful money consciousness.

Pay Attention to the Energy You Surround Yourself With

In this component, you will be paying attention to the energy that you surround yourself with. Make every effort to avoid negative and toxic people in conversations. If you find yourself around negative energy and people, make an effort to excuse yourself and to get away from those situations.

Start spending more time with people who are positive and who are striving to achieve the type of life that you are as well. It's also very beneficial to spend time with people that are further advanced than you. To surround yourself with positive mentors like myself.

This book gives you the exact steps that you need to follow to attract money fast. While utilizing the steps and strategies within this book you will want to capitalize your Attract Money Fast Routine by staying away from negative things and negative people.

In order to develop a powerful money

consciousness to attract abundance and prosperity you want to surround yourself with people who are already have a prosperity consciousness. Energetic vibrational frequencies tend to synchronize to each other. This means that when you surround yourself with prosperous thinking people, you too will become prosperous.

As you focus in on the energy around you your awareness will improve, and you will be able to quickly feel whether or not the energy is good for you to surround yourself with. Eventually you may be letting some people go in your life. Negative people that do nothing but bring you down should not be in your life. If it's a family member, then you can limit your exposure to that person.

Take Time Each Day to Imagine and Dream

To entertain your imagination is to allow for the successful expansion of your money consciousness. Taking time each day to imagine and dream situations where you are immensely wealthy and are attracting money fast, will help you to expand your money consciousness.

One powerful strategy in regards to imagining and dreaming, is to create a vision board for yourself. This is simply images and pictures of things that you desire to achieve in your life in the near coming future.

Having a vision board gives you a model in which you can take some time each day to imagine and dream as if you already have these possessions in your reality. This particular component only requires a couple of minutes each day.

The best times are first thing in the morning, and the last thing before you go to sleep, to look at your vision board and to expand your imagination on experiencing your ideal life and attracting money to you fast.

Most people that use vision boards and stay consistent, on a daily basis, with focusing on the images on their vision boards, usually wind up manifesting those things into their lives.

So, a vision board is a very powerful tool and this component of imagining and dreaming your ideal life is a very powerful method for expanding your money consciousness to allow for more abundance and prosperity to flow into your life.

Understanding that as you follow your Attract Money Fast Routine, you will be developing your money consciousness. More importantly, you will begin to realize that everything that you think and feel and what you expose yourself to any outside world, will be a contribution towards your total consciousness.

The more you are aware of this truth of the development of consciousness, the more you will be cautious on what thoughts, feelings, and outside world influences you will expose yourself to from now on.

Your ability to carefully construct and develop your consciousness through your thoughts, feelings, actions, and what you expose yourself in the outside world, will determine how powerful of a money consciousness you will have.

So be cautious of what you feed your mind because your mind is always feeding your consciousness, and your consciousness is always determining what you're going to experience in your near future.

Now let's move the chapter 9 where you can begin to set up your Attract Money Fast Routine and begin to follow it on a daily basis to allow yourself to attract money fast.

Chapter 9

Your Attract Money Fast Routine

"Everything is energy and that is all there is to it. Match the frequency of the reality you want and you cannot help but get that reality. It can be no other way. This is not philosophy. This is physics

— Albert Einstein

In this chapter you will learn precisely how to create and follow your Attract Money Fast Routine. We are going to go over each component, step, and strategy for you to follow to outline and begin your routine for attracting money fast.

First, I will list each strategy for you to follow, and then I will go into each strategy, to explain the steps which you will follow, to fully utilize each strategy, to maximize your routine to achieve maximum results.

Once you have completed this chapter you will know exactly how to successfully conduct your Attract Money Fast Routine. You can then begin your daily process of implementing your Attract Money Fast Routine.

Let's Get Started!

Step 1

Your Money Goals and Money Intention

The first step in your Attract Money Fast Routine is to establish your money goals and your money intention. In chapter 1, you established your money goal list. You then established your money intention. Your money intention is going to be your primary focus. Utilizing the steps and strategies within this routine, you will have single pointed to focus on your money intention.

To get great ideas in creating your money intention refer back to the examples of money intentions in chapter 1. Those examples will help you to come up with a powerful money intention which you will focus on utilizing the strategies within this daily routine.

Step 2

Mastering the Principles of Attracting Money

In step two you will be mastering the principles that are laid out and explained in Chapter 2. The best way to master these principles is to get some 3 x 5 cards and write down the principles on the cards.

You can then review the cards regularly to memorize the principles so they become imprinted into your subconscious mind. Mastering these principles will allow you to carry yourself in the most successful manner in maximizing the process of attracting money fast.

Each step in this routine is just as important to the overall process of attracting money fast. After I cover each step, I will give you a sample day in which you can conduct a successful Attract Money Fast Routine.

Step 3

Attracting Money with Your Subconscious Mind

Your subconscious mind is your most powerful tool to attract money fast. In chapter 3 we talked about the most effective ways to program your subconscious mind. To repeat the word "Wealth", or "More Money" over and over again. Especially before you go to sleep.

The subconscious is programmed best through repetition. Repeating single words feeds the subconscious mind with your desire to allow your subconscious mind to then bring about that particular desire into your physical reality.

The next strategy to program your subconscious mind, to attract money fast, is to feel as if you are now receiving large amounts of money. The feeling is the secret. The subconscious mind functions in emotional energized frequencies of energy. Words and emotionalized feelings are the two components that allow you to maximize the programming of your subconscious mind for your subconscious mind to deliver to you the things that you desire.

The words symbolize what you desire in the physical world. The emotional charged frequency of feeling, gives you the ability to vibrate at a frequency which commands the subconscious mind to deliver back to you the circumstances and experiences that match that frequency.

We talked about gratitude and how being grateful and appreciative is an emotional charged frequency of energy which the subconscious mind receives and then manifests physical experiences that bring more gratitude and appreciative experiences in your life.

Another component of the subconscious mind is for you to feel you deserve the thing that you want to manifest into your life. When you feel you deserve a thing that thing will more than likely be manifested through your subconscious mind.

Then we talked about imagination which is another powerful strategy for programming your subconscious mind. To maximize step number 3, refer to Chapter 3 to compile these steps for you to follow. With imagination, you can utilize the bolded examples of imagination which I provided for you.

The rich get richer because the subconscious mind of a rich person is filled with money, abundance, and all things good. As long as you can successfully start the momentum of thinking rich, feeling rich, and acting rich, you can start the energetic momentum of becoming rich and wealthy.

More importantly, you could begin the process of the rich getting richer. As long as you are consistent and persistent, and stay the course, you can build this momentum starting today and throughout the rest of your life and maximize your ability to attract money fast now and for the rest of your life.

Step 4

Feel to Attract Money Fast

Feeling is an extremely powerful strategy in attracting money fast. The process of healing your way to attracting money fast is a process of momentum which grows as you are consistent with it.

In your Attract Money Fast Routine, you will be spending at least 30 minutes per day undisturbed, and focused on the feelings of how you would feel if you already had a large amount of money in your bank account.

The feeling is the emotion which sends the signal out into the universe. The emotionally charged feeling is the energetic frequency of communication with your subconscious mind and with the universe as a whole. Your ability to build and expand your feelings of having large amounts of money will maximize your ability to attract money fast.

Step 5

Attracting Money with Affirmations and Self-Talk

In chapter 5 and chapter 6 we covered how to successfully utilize affirmations and self-talk. In your Attract Money Fast Routine you will be using affirmations and self-talk to successfully allow you to attract money fast. In chapters 5 and 6 there are examples of affirmations and self-talk statements that you can utilize, in your Attract Money Fast Routine.

Once I cover these steps I will give you a sample day of utilizing the steps to maximize your Attract Money Fast Routine.

Step 6

Money Gratitude and Appreciation

In chapter 7, we talked about money, gratitude, and appreciation. Gratitude and appreciation are powerful attracting emotions that attract all things good into your life. Make sure that you have read chapter 7 thoroughly, and understand the importance of gratitude and appreciation, in your ability to attract money fast.

Step 7

The Development of Your Money Consciousness

Your Money consciousness is the accumulation of your thoughts, feelings, and especially your belief systems in relations to money. You will be developing your money consciousness through following the steps within this Attract Money Fast Routine.

Remember the most important components of developing your money consciousness.

1. Pay attention to your thoughts and words

2. Pay attention to the energy you surround yourself with

3. Take time each day to imagine and dream.

Below is a sample or an example of a daily routine of attracting money fast. You can use this example as a model for you to create the best routine for yourself. You don't have to follow this particular example step-by-step. You can instead rearrange and change things as you see fit.

Sample Day

Attracting Money Fast Routine

1. In the morning you will review your money goals and your money intention.

2. For five minutes you'll repeat your selected affirmations. You can record your affirmations and play them back to listen to them at least 5 to 10 minutes per day. Affirmations are best utilized first thing in the morning and last thing before you go to sleep.

3. Throughout the day you will repeat your self-talk statement. Throughout the day there will be segments for example, taking a shower, commuting in your car, shopping at the grocery store, and picking up the kids at school if you have kids. In these segments you will remind yourself to speak your self-talk statements which will empower yourself, and your ability, to attract

money fast.

4. In the early afternoon or early evening you will set aside 30 to 45 minutes, or an hour if you can and do your most powerful strategy of the day. This strategy consists of being in an undisturbed place, while listening to relaxing music of your choice preferably with headphones, and focusing on your money intention.

5. While you are focusing on your money intention, you will be focusing on the feelings of already having a large amount of money in your bank account the gratitude and appreciation of already having this large amount of money, and while doing this, you will be growing and developing your ability to cast your energetic emotionalize feeling frequency out into the universe.

Note: Step number four is the most important step in your Attract Money Fast Routine. The ability for you to be undisturbed and to focus on the feelings and gratitude of having large amounts of money in your life, give you the ability to send the signal of energetic abundance to the universe.

6. Imagination, and utilizing your vision board of images that you want to manifest into your life expands your imagination to allow your imagination to grow, which will grow your perception of reality of what's possible. The best times to utilize your imagination is first thing in the morning and last thing before you go to sleep.

7. Set aside 15 minutes to go over the principles of attracting money which you learned about in chapter 2. Utilize 3 x 5 index cards to write down these principles so you can review them on a daily basis to memorize and to imprint them into your subconscious mind. You can do this while watching TV in the evening or you can do this anytime you have some free time.

8. However, you want to make sure that you go over the principles on your 3 x 5 index cards every day until they become a full habitual understanding. The importance of these principles becoming a habitual understanding, will allow your subconscious mind to develop the habits for you, in your daily actions, to maximize the principles, which will allow you to attract money fast.

9. The final step which is automatic, through the six steps prior to this, you will be developing your money consciousness. Each step is equally important and especially step number four which is of vital importance for you to do on a daily basis.

Go over the example above of the seven steps of your Attract Money Fast Routine. Depending on your schedule find the best time to do step number four. The other steps are relatively easy to fit in throughout the day. Affirmations and vision boards along with expanding imagination, are best to do first thing in the morning and last thing before you go to sleep.

The Critical Factors, and the most important components of the attract money fast routine are Persistence and Consistency

As I mentioned a few times throughout this book, in order for you to attract money fast, you must be consistent every day in following your Attract Money Fast Routine. You have to ignite the momentum of energy to allow for new and expanded experiences to manifest into your life.

In regards to attracting money fast, as you follow this routine and increase your energetic frequency, sending out higher and higher frequencies of feeling as if you are rich and wealthy right now, your signal will be consistent and gradually growing stronger. **This is the true work to attract money fast.**

Of course, you will need to put some work into

your physical actions to line up the people, circumstances, and events to allow for money to come into your physical experience.

But the bottom line is, when your energy is vibrating at the frequencies of gratitude, appreciation, financial abundance, financial freedom, and having the life that you want and the feelings of having it now, this frequency is what will maximize your ability to attract money fast.

Now we will move to the bonus chapter in which I will teach you the initial steps to money mastery. This is an important chapter which will allow you to know the importance of initial resources that are required for gaining financial freedom and financial abundance in the physical world.

Bonus Chapter

The Initial Steps to Money Mastery

Congratulations! You now know the secrets to attracting money fast. Make sure that you utilize and maximize your daily routine and the steps and strategies, that I covered in the previous chapters, to allow yourself to attract money fast.

In this bonus chapter, I am going to give you the initial steps to mastering money. In the physical world the ability to master money of course is your ability to make it. More importantly, your ability to strategically use money that you have accumulated, as a tool, to begin to allow that money to work for you.

The number one goal in achieving financial freedom is for you to begin to save money. The easiest way to save money is to earn more than you spend. Many people are just getting by financially. You may be one of these people. You have bills, expenses and things that you have to pay for every month. And it usually seems that no matter how much you make you can't seem to save any money.

The most powerful initial step to money mastery is your ability to increase your income. If your current job has a limitation on income you will want to expand your ability to create a secondary income.

The Internet has many different opportunities for you to make money. If you were to spend your free time exploring different opportunities you can realize that there is a lot of opportunity out there for you to begin to create a secondary income stream. This particular secondary income will give you the ability to begin the process of saving money to then allow that money begin to work for you.

There is one hindrance that gets in the way in many people's ability to start making money online. Lack of knowledge, lack of skills, and the inability to know the exact steps and components to generate money, through any opportunity online.

Think of the world of making money opportunities as a pyramid structure. What I mean by pyramid structure is not the scam you hear about on the news, but a structure of hierarchy of knowledge and wisdom, in the art of making large amounts of money.

In a pyramid there are levels. Think of the low-level as people who have no idea of what they need to do in order to make money with online money-making opportunities. The next level could be an example of a person that knows how to make $10,000 per month. The next level of the pyramid could be someone that knows how to make $50,000 per month. And so forth up each level.

The point I am making is the secrets of self-investment. When you invest in yourself, in education and information that helps you to advance to the next level, you symbolically move to the next level in the pyramid structure.

There are people that know more than you. By simply investing in yourself, you give yourself the empowerment to advance up the pyramid structure, in which you can then educate others and earn larger amounts of income.

This pyramid structure, is a metaphor for personal empowerment, and your ability to maximize your ability to make large amounts of money, and to achieve your goals and dreams.

So how can you make a quick jump from the bottom level of the pyramid and structure to the next level, for example, where you learn and know exactly how to make $10,000 per month, with an online business?

One of the most powerful Internet business opportunities is one that is turnkey. You don't want to waste time and money waiting until you finally have set up your own business, when you can easily jump in and utilize a turnkey business, to begin to establish your secondary income.

I personally utilize a turnkey business that is a

high ticket direct sales online business. This business opportunity allows a member to make $3500 up to $22,500 per sale.

This type of business is the perfect secondary income that you can build quickly. Most online business opportunities including selling products and services at retail prices of $10-$97 as an example, require hundreds to thousands of sales to accumulate a lot of money.

High ticket direct sales business opportunities give you the ability to generate money at a much quicker rate, which gives you the ability to establish the money momentum that you need to achieve financial freedom.

Now a business like this, may not be for everyone. However, I can tell you that I have done extremely well with this business model and it has rapidly progressed me well in my own personal accumulation of wealth.

So, the purpose of this bonus chapter is for you to explore this high ticket direct sales opportunity. This could be a perfect fit for you to create a large secondary income.

The ability to achieve money mastery is to establish a very powerful financial foundation. The quicker you can build this foundation through saving money and building capital, the more money you have to start working for you.

To learn more about this high ticket direct sales business opportunity simply join our mailing list at my main website below.

www.tsfisher.com

Conclusion

Attracting money fast is simply aligning yourself with the energy of financial abundance and gratitude. Utilizing the steps and strategies within this book, you will be working on your routine, on a daily basis, to align yourself with the energy of attracting money fast.

I hope you enjoyed reading this book and I advise you to reread this book and to specifically outline and begin your Attract Money Fast Routine.

The bonus chapter was added to give you an opportunity to create a strong secondary income stream. In order to achieve financial freedom, you need to have extra money coming in each month for you to save.

Saving money is the starting point of all wealth and abundance. As you save money, you then have the ability, to have that money begin to work for you. Once you have enough money working for you, you can then have the ability to achieve financial freedom.

One of the best ways to save money is to establish a secondary income. In the bonus chapter, you can learn more about the direct sales high ticket business that I am involved with. I can show you exactly how it works and exactly how to maximize your ability to earn money within the business opportunity. Refer back to the bonus chapter and join my mailing list at my main website, and I will give you more information about the business opportunity.

In my book, **"The 11 Secret Power Codes of Getting Rich"**, I cover more of the physical steps to become rich and wealthy. Definitely check out that book, and get a copy, so you can master the teachings within this book here, and 11 secret power codes, which help you to master the outside work in becoming rich and wealthy.

Please leave us a good review of this book on Amazon. If you utilize the steps and strategies within this book you will indeed attract money fast. The only thing I need from you in return is a good review of this book on Amazon. I completely appreciate it!

Visit my websites below and I hope we can do more business together. I am here to help you achieve your goals and dreams.

Abundantly,

Thomas Fisher
www.tsfisher.com

About the Author

Thomas Fisher is one of the most interesting and inspiring life transformation specialists in the personal development and metaphysical community.

He is famous for delivering very unique and informative training strategies, in specific variations, to maximize your learned knowledge and application of the mastery of success, financial abundance, and personal happiness.

Delivering results is the bottom line for Thomas, and Thomas stands behind his message to make sure you achieve maximized results in the pursuit and accomplishment of your goals and dreams.

Finally, you have access to a professional mentor that delivers exclusively rare breakthrough strategies, to ensure your maximum understanding and application of the principals of success, in a direct and easy way to understand and apply.

As a true contrarian, Thomas delivers cutting edge books and audio programs which deliver the hidden and mysterious secrets of success, allowing you to achieve the life you deeply desire.

Thomas has invested 1000's of hours, reading over 1000+ books and audio programs on personal development, success, metaphysics, personal finance, business, skill sets, and health related materials.

You can now gain the unfair advantage by hiring Thomas as your personal success mentor, delivering the most exciting and sometimes even some of the most forbidden strategies for fast success!

Stay in Touch with Thomas

Main Website

www.tsfisher.com

***

Social Media

Facebook: Facebook.com/tsfisher7

YouTube: Youtube.com/user/theopulentmind

Instagram: Instagram.com/theopulentlife

Twitter: Twitter.com/opulent7

***

Amazon Author Page

www.opulentbooks.com